MAKING CHILD SMART

VISHNU SEKHAR

*"Education is the manifestation
of perfection already in men."*

-Swami Vivekananda

Foreword[1]

What prompted me to write a self-help book like this is my disillusionment as a teacher with thousands of parents and their crude parenting methodologies. I knew that as a psychologist and counsellor I had to do something fruitful to improve contemporary parenting, and that is how I came to the idea of bringing up this book.

As far as learning parenting skills is goes, we learn them from our own parents. However, parenting styles of our parents may not be right as they might have just followed the wrong methods of their own parents. All the parents I have met so far, with the exception of one or two, in spite of high education and reputed jobs, are found to be lacking right parenting skills, though their intention is always to help children build a future. Unfortunately, methods they have used are not empowering but are downgrading. Their decisions are more emotional than scientific.

The ideas discussed in this book are backed by my own successful employment of them in my life as a father. All parents, however, must reflect themselves for a while with patience while implementing the techniques implicitly narrated in the book. The easiest thing to do is to neglect it with numerous excuses. However, the deepest satisfaction of raising a smart child, in all sense, is that it is the greatest work parents can do in their lifetimes. Best wishes.

PART I INFANT

A child is born. The very change in the environment from the mother's womb to that of the outside world makes the child cry. The baby immediately senses a change—an uncomfortable change. It is painful for, like all of us, to lose one's comfort zone. The very moment his sense organs collect information and send it to the brain, the baby wonders what these sensations are: heat, cold, sound, smell, and sight. The brain starts to make sense of this information (Perception). When the baby is covered with soft wool and laid in the cradle with utmost care, the child's brain takes it as a safe and cosy place.

Later, the fifth sense organ, the tongue, makes up for the sufferings caused by the other four. The baby finds something soothing and sweet and thinks, "Wow! It is very tasty. Let me have it more and more. It removes all the pain I am suffering from. Great." This way, the baby learns the first lesson: "Over all other sense organs, the one situated in my mouth is the best because it brings sweet memories."

The infant begins to learn the "pain pleasure principle"—avoid pain and get pleasure. The infant cries when he does not get the warmth from others. He knows it is not safe to be lying alone. Hearing him cry, others come and take him and caress him; he feels the warmth of touch and stops crying. If it is his mother, he uses his inherited abilities to suck milk and learns the practicability of cry to avoid pain and get what he wants. This way, the infant learns his first ethereal lesson of habit formation.

The baby learns the smell of milk and associates it with his mother. That is why a crying baby calms down the very moment the mother takes him in her hand. The infant has already learnt to differentiate his mother from others by smell. The baby also listens to the playful voices of elders and differentiates their pitch and tone. He associates this with different people negatively or positively. During this stage, the sense of smell and hearing are more developed than that of sight.

Sometimes, parents get irritated by infant's cries, especially at midnight when they are sound asleep. If he is attended each time he cries, the baby learns that he is at a safe place surrounded by caring and dependable people. If nobody attends him, he assumes that he is in an unknown land with untrustworthy people. The two sense organs to be stimulated at this stage are the sense of touch and the sense of taste. The more the parents satisfy this condition, the happier the children grow up. Take them, touch them, caress them, and kiss them. Play some games that involve a lot of cuddling and caressing. Provide them with ample food till they feel satisfied, which in the case of infants, is always mother's milk.

If these two organs of touch and taste are not fully satisfied during infant-hood, the child will be fixated on these. Later in childhood and adulthood, these suppressed desires for food and touch may exhibit as greed and inappropriate attention seeking behaviour that are condemned in all societies. We witness such individuals in our society. We often label them as an elephant, a pig, or a glutton. Touch deficiency during infant-hood may prompt children to seek attention at inappropriate occasions, and they may get rejected further, which may lead to various personality disorders during adulthood.

Summary

A new born babies' emotional needs to be cared for and milk should be fulfilled preferentially. This forms the foundation for children to successfully step to the next developmental stages and grow a healthy personality. It is unfortunate that these days parents don't take this seriously due to lack of time or unwillingness due to self-consciousness and selfishness.

PART II EXPLORATION

After many months of lying in the cradle and being handled by elders, the baby tries to crawl. He moves around to explore his surroundings. The baby partially notices the objects around him and learns to adapt his eyesight. He recognises different shapes, sizes, and colours. If his tongue has been sensitised by others so far, now is the time to put it to use. He reaches objects around him and tastes them based on the information stored through the tongue that all things are edible. His journey begins here—the most important stage of his life.

<u>TO BE OR NOT TO BE</u>

A baby is born with 300 billion neurones. Neurones are brain nerve cells that design and decide a child's future. They are like yarns in clothes; the quality of yarn decides the quality of the cloth. More neurones a child has, more intelligent he can become. However, after birth, with time, the number of neurones declines drastically. The body retains only those neurones that are essential for the child to master and survive in the environment. If the environment is complex and difficult to master, the child needs to utilise more neurones to store more information and develop complex skills. A baby born in a forest thousands of years ago needed to use his neurones to overcome the dangers lurking in the forest. To achieve this, he had to master the whole fauna and flora and the unwritten rules being followed by his community and other animals in the jungle. In addition, he had to have sharpened physical skills, like running, jumping, climbing, and swimming with lightning fast speed.

Unused neurones die and disappear through a process called synaptic pruning to increase the efficiency of the existing neural network. Imagine the super human skills a forester might have developed to survive in a forest—alertness, dexterity, strength, and agility. Even a five-time Olympic champion could not have beaten a forester in any of the events of the former's choice. The secrets of the extraordinary capabilities of a forager lie in his optimum utilisation of neurones for these specific tasks that help him survive in the forest.

A new neurone is like a computer chip. Any information, negative or positive, useful or useless, can be stored in it and manipulated as per our need. So, from the 300 billion neurones at birth, the child retains the neurones that he utilises to learn something new. To achieve maximum retention of neurones, the child should be abundantly exposed to his surroundings to explore it.

Exposure is the key, whether it is a natural environment, artificial, or simulated. Unfortunately, a modern child is confined to the four walls of a flat—truly a barren place for the child's intellectual, social, and emotional development.

In the past, when people lived in communities, a child had a lot of free space and ample opportunities to experience nature and learn the behaviour of many people with different temperaments, attitudes, abilities, and beliefs, which helped humans to develop their brain faster leading to stupendous advancement of the present generation. However, a child living in a flat is destined to see the same people and objects in the same place every day. The child crawls to furniture in the house, touches it, licks it, and smells it. "Familiarity breeds contempt", and soon, the child gets bored with these and gets frustrated, like a thirsty elephant who has seen a pot of water. He needs only a small percentage of neurones to store this little information. The remaining neurones in the brain deteriorate rapidly through neurotic pruning. This child will have lost half of his neurones by the time he joins kindergarten at the age of three. Luckily, the remaining neurones are sufficient enough to become a hero!

So during this stage of exploration, all children look seemingly vibrant with a lot of energy in a wobbling body. The body will take its own time to become stable though the brain is not so. It is stimulated when you touch him, cuddle with him, talk to him, smile at him, and gift him anything new. The most important activity during this stage is communication. Spend as much time as possible to talk with your child. The child may not understand you fully, but every new sound you make is a new experience to him. All these sounds are not in vain; they will be registered in his brain. Talking to the child is one of the easiest and most effective ways to stimulate the child's brain. Good parents do it though it is a boring work to them because they understand the difference it can make to the cognitive development of their child. Introduce as many languages as possible to the child early. Indian children are lucky in this respect as almost all are born in bilingual families. In my family, my mother speaks Malayalam, my father speaks Hindi, my wife speaks Tamil, and I speak English. This causes the child to stimulate more neurones to process these different sounds.

Bring the child out from the four wall-enclosure, show him the sky, plants, trees, birds, and butterflies and explain their whereabouts. The child may only moan and giggle at you when you say all this, but they are learning something in their own way, which will not be in vain. If possible, give him a new experience every day. Keep all his five senses busy.

For those parents who live in flats, virtual reality educational applications can be used. Fortunately, our brain has no ability to distinguish between a real and an unreal world. Whatever is thrown to it, it assumes it as real. That is why, we shiver and sweat when we see a horrible dream.

 A child who is given ample opportunities to explore the surroundings freely will develop the capacity to process information faster and do complex tasks related to space, shape, and size like a civil engineer who visualises images of a building before constructing it. Children who are encouraged to play various psychomotor games (any games that involve a lot physical movements) will make his country proud of him later as an Olympic Gold medallist.

You may have noticed that some children start thinking and doing things quickly: they begin to laugh before you slip on a banana leaf as communication among neurones is so fast that they have already processed the image of your fall.

Parents who interact with their children regularly are making future linguists. A child who is encouraged to solve problems will later be able to solve the mysteries of life and matter. A child who is taught to distinguish between real and unreal, truth and untruth, original and fake, and superstitions and science will develop reasoning skills. Early introduction of numbers can develop numerical intelligence. Patience and perseverance pay. Encourage children to count peanuts before popping them into their mouth. Let him count the number of bites he takes to eat a banana. Gradually introduce toys that teach simple maths like addition and subtraction. Shakunthala Devi, popularly known as the human computer, is an example of the unlimited possibilities of the human brain. Just at the age of three, her father introduced her to the wonders of numbers. He trained her every day and facilitated her inborn talent to remember and calculate numbers with incredulous speed. Her success story shows the importance of early identification of a child's aptitude. Imagine what would have happened to her if she had followed her father's profession in circus.

When a curious child is introduced to new and various experiences every day, his muscles become stronger and stronger with hardship, and the brain too strengthens its cells to cope with life's demands. The child will first be perplexed with numerous colours, shapes, movements, and feelings. Every first experience is vaguely stored in his nerve cells. Constant exposure to various experiences strengthens the intensity of impulses stored in the brain. It is like colouring a picture; with every coat, the intensity of the colour increases. As the child grows older, he adds more and more information to his long-term memory. With every new information, concepts regarding people, world, and himself become clearer to him. Now, we can imagine the long journey made by organisms to reach the stage of evolution we see today. Some important information that is necessary for survival of a species is passed to their offsprings through an organ with a coding mechanism called genes. Some information is deleted and some is added, and the journey continues.

The child makes meaning of the plethora of information stored in his brain when neurones communicate each other. A neurone is connected with other neurones through a tube-like nerve fibre called axons. When a neurone is connected with only a single neurone, the so-called brain power is low; when it is connected with many neurones that store a variety of information, the brain power is high. It is analogous to a single computer and a network of computers. The latter has access to more information and can process it faster.

The secret of brain power lies in two factors: how much information neurones carry and how many axon branches are formed to link them. When a child is engaged in challenging tasks, he makes use of internal genetic information and external learnt information. Each attempt by the child towards a task, despite the outcome, is a step forward in his intellectual capabilities. Thomas Alva Edison's life story of the invention of the electric bulb is an example of unfaltering optimism and perseverance. Edison failed hundreds of times before he successfully made the bulb. How did it happen? All his failures were stepping stones to success. With each failure, he learnt new ideas about the working of the electric bulb. He based his insight on this new information that nobody else in the world happened to know because nobody had ever made his unique errors.

There is no limit to the capacity of the brain. It can grow like a banyan tree as long as it receives adequate nourishment. Give your child ample opportunities to solve different problems. (To a child, every new experience is a new problem when he curiously tries to make meaning out of it.) Even the first smile you have gifted him is a grave problem to him. That is why he just frowned to you at the time. Gradually, he learns the meaning of a smile in conjunction with some sounds, pats, kisses, and milk as a sign of affection and well-being. Later, he too will do the same and gift you with smiles, joyful giggles, and vibrations.

When a child is challenged with a problem, he will try to analyse the problem with the data already stored in his brain. When the process is repeated, a miracle happens—myelination. Axons, the tiny hands of neurones that help neurones communicate among themselves are deposited with a substance called myelin. It is like electroplating. A sheath is formed over axons that enables them to send and receive information faster. The end result is a more powerful brain. More challenges a child goes through in his formative years, stronger the brain grows and a true genius is created.

The future of children is in the hands of parents. A neglected child grows into an ordinary person. However, a child who is cared for, attended, loved, and respected will grow into an intelligent person. So challenge them, caress them, communicate with them, play with them, but never neglect them. Give them ample opportunities to explore the world. He may appear to be a nuisance at many occasions, but bear with it if you are serious regarding the development of your child. You need time and patience to achieve it. Parenting is a serious job like any other—you need to work hard with patience keeping the goal in mind.

Neglecting a child in his formative years and then cursing him for his future failures is ironic. You are the creator. You are the caretaker. You can build your child as you wish. A child to a parent is like clay in the hands of a potter. Remember, every child is born with the potential to become a hero. Albert Einstein was certified as a hopeless incompetent by his principal and teachers when he was a student. It was his mother's stern belief in her son that made him a genius. Trust your child. Believe in him. Be patient with him. Forgive him. If you can do this, one day, your child will make you proud for the trust and patience you have shown him.

From Floor to Feet

A child who is trying to explore his surroundings should not be disdained from doing so. He should be encouraged to investigate the outside world. This is a natural tendency in every living being to master its environment as survival depends on how fast an animal can adapt. Human babies also have the same tendency—learn faster, grow faster, and master faster. Till one year old, he has been lying somewhere helplessly, dreaming of butterflies, but with time, he learns to crawl and stand on his feet. He begins to run from one place to another, observing objects around him, touching them, and studying the various features to ensure that they are malleable before swallowing them. His inherited tendency to be autonomous will prompt him to make his own choices. His natural tendency to explore, assess, and decide should be encouraged to explore infinite possibilities. It does not mean unchecked wandering of the child among life threatening objects. Even a small piece of pebble can choke a child to death.

Parents can create a safe environment at home by removing tiny household items away from children before allowing them to move around freely. This ensures that their instinct to learn is not curtailed. They learn to learn themselves. Later, they will show enthusiasm and spirit to go deep into the matters of things and mysteries of creation and share their insights from their unique points of view.

The explorative period is the most important time in the life of a child. It is in this period that children form basic ideas about all concrete things and abstract ideas. It is true that every child is born with some information encoded in his genes that is a result of years of evolution and is passed from one generation to other. For example, a child possesses different emotions, like love, anger, excitement, disgust, and joy, even at the time of birth, which have developed over time since the development of human beings thousands of years ago. New information, whether emotions or skills, that helps members of a species to survive in their environment, has been encoded in our genes by being passed from one generation to the next. For example, our ancestors, the foragers, needed information about the flora and fauna of the region they lived in. To achieve this, sharp attention and listening skills like a rabbit, strong and agile limbs like a chimpanzee, heightened olfactory capabilities like a fox were developed over time. But, these animalistic capabilities were not enough for a human to surpass all other animals. Our bigger brains were capable of producing and managing emotions, like fear, anger, pain, hunger, joy, and love—fear for the dangerous predators and natural calamities, anger for defence and escape, pain for self-help, hunger for survival, joy for success, and love for family and community. Like this, many other skills and abilities have developed over time and transferred to the offsprings through a complex coding mechanism called genes. The information encoded in genes changes from time to time as per needs. Any changes that are necessary for the survival of living beings are developed, recorded, and transferred. For the same reason, any useless information is discarded over time.

Humans have been living in groups for thousands of years. Naturally, emotions like love, compassion, hatred, disgust, anger, sadness, and joy have become the essential qualities for humans to live in a community. These qualities are not found in other animals in such complex forms and distinguish us from them. Though a lioness loves and looks after her cubs, she will neither try to maintain a lifelong relationship with them or when they are old, complain of her cubs' ingratitude.

These unique human emotions we see in their present form are a result of millions of years of evolution. They are embedded in the genes of each one of us. In the same way, various abilities and skills have also developed through man's continuous struggle against unpredictable nature.

From the history of human evolution, we get clues about why people have different abilities though they are born in the same place at the same time. We say every child is born with divinity. Vivekananda Swami has said, "Education is the manifestation of perfection already in man." It is absolutely true from evolutionary psychology. Every child is born with infinite capabilities developed as a result of evolution. Every child is born with information encoded in his DNA in a hundred billion neurones. This potential can be tapped and nourished through selective exposure and stimulation of a child's brain.

Lazlo Polgar, the father of Edith Polgar, a chess prodigy, believed that any child can be made exceptional in a subject by early introduction to that subject. To prove this, he gave rigorous chess training to his three daughters Edith, Susan, and Sophia at the cost of school education. Despite criticism from the government and the society, Lazlo Polgar persisted with his experiment; finally, all his daughters received the honour of Grand Master and International Master Titles. How did it happen? If we speak biologically, the early training paved the way for strengthening the neurones and their axons, all for the sole purpose of solving chess problems in the case of Edith Polgar. The same can be replicated with any child in diverse fields. Parents can make their children doctors, engineers, or scientists.

Fill a child's mind with love and affection, and he will love his fellow beings; rejoice with him when he smiles, and he will strive to make others smile; empathise with him when he cries, and he will feel a heavy heart when he sees the sufferings of others; speak with him assertively, and he will learn the art of communication; share new thoughts with him, and thoughtfulness will develop in him; narrate him the stories of human struggles against evils, and he will be determined to protect his brothers; develop his observation skills; and appreciate him abundantly when he learns something new.

Let your child freely explore the world, be logical, and be patience with his doubts.

Parents often make the mistake of telling ghost stories to children as a shortcut to make them obedient. They say, "Don't cry or the witch will turn you into a snake." These types of unreal stories distort the child's thinking very early. Albert Einstein used to question his teachers when he heard illogical ideas from them. A child raised in a superstitious atmosphere may remain foolish all through his life as a result of his undeveloped critical, analytical, and logical thinking skills.

Foragers' children may have been smarter than our kids are. Imagine how difficult it was for a child to survive amid dangers at every nook and corner of a jungle. Naturally, he learnt faster and memorised everything he came across sharply because it was literally a matter of life and death. A petty error in calculation may make him a prey to predators. Every moment from birth to death was a challenge for him. Whole life was an experience to them. Then, it is not very surprising to know that our foraging ancestors' brains were larger than ours are.

On the contrary, our child is born in a safe and cosy environment, cuddled and protected by well-wishers. He is fed everything, and doesn't need to use his inherited capabilities for anything. No wonder the average IQ of contemporary children is decreasing day by day.

Intelligence is proportionate to the total work done by the brain. The more complicated the task is, the more agility the brain develops. These tasks done over time become permanently recorded in the DNA and are passed to the new generation. According to needs, the brain either gets up or loses its power. A combination of data inherited and data received from environment helps humans survive in the world.

Therefore, the best time to strengthen the brain is when it has more neurones. During the exploratory stage (1–3 age group), children possess 100 billion neurones. Through challenging tasks, these billion potentials can be utilised to their optimum capacities.

Though every child can develop into anybody, our aim should

be to make him the best in a particular field. Through rigorous training, any child can become an artist, engineer, or doctor, but may not be the best in the world. To become the best, early discovery of a child's aptitude (inherited abilities) is crucial. On the contrary, parents these days press children to choose subjects of their choice and pursue a career they had dreamt of, which are often the unfulfilled desires of their parents. A child born to become a singer and trained to become a doctor will only become a mediocre doctor. Every child should be helped to identify his inherited skills and trained accordingly. The DNA a human carries forward is the result of millions of years of evolution, which cannot be duplicated in a mere 20 years or in a man's lifetime. Instead, if these 20–30 years are spent to further develop the inherited talent of children, the world will grow faster.

Inborn talents can be identified by observing children closely. Shakunthala Devi's father noticed her exceptional numerical abilities very early. Rest is history. She mesmerised the world with her superhuman math skill, getting the nick name "the human computer".

Parents have to constantly observe the behaviours of their children and keep a note of them. Often, children show interest in the abilities that they are born with. It doesn't mean interest is always a sign of aptitude. A child may show a lot of interest in drawing pictures but may not have the aptitude for it. A child may be passionate about music but may not have the talent to sing.

"Every child is born an artist. The problem is how to remain an artist once we grow up." In schools, children are taught various subjects, often compelling them to excel in all subjects. This method is unscientific and won't work with majority of children; they struggle with these subjects. Teachers and parents segregate them as "weak children" or "slow bloomers". In future, they become what their teachers, friends, and parents name them— an average human being. Numerous children may have ended up without realising their inborn potentialities in their life.

The problem is that our educational institutions operate on social expectations and are not based on reality and truth. As a consequence, all parents want their children to become doctors and engineers not because their children are talented but because these jobs are lucrative. In this rat race, the child's inner world and hidden talents are completely ignored. The child remains perplexed and confused all through his life with the belief that he was born incompetent. The confusion is between external illusion and internal reality. Shankar Mahadevan is a renowned Bollywood singer and studied to become a software engineer before discovering his hidden musical skills. J. K. Rowling, Kathryn Joosten, Peter Mark Roget, Vera Wang, and Joy Behar are some celebrities who realised their talent late in their life.

In today's Internet era, everything is sunk in fantasy, and truth has become illusory. In such a world, parents, who are entrusted with the responsibility to take final decisions with regard to their children's future, must help children realise their actual worth rather than give in to fate and destiny. A religious person calls it a heavenly gift; an atheist calls it an inborn talent; an evolutionary psychologist calls it an inherited aptitude.

<u>SUMMARY</u>

Therefore, the time when children begin to slowly explore the world is of paramount importance. This is the time the organ decides how many neurones are to be retained to advance life in a particular environment. Maximum exploration of children's faculties through simple tasks, activities, and language can help preserving maximum number of neurones for future use. Research shows that the total number of neurones in our brain at the time of birth become half by the time we reach the age of three. The death of neurones can be minimised only through constant exposure of children to age-appropriate, challenging, and meaningful tasks. Another critical change that occurs at this stage is the formation of axons and the myelination process. More neurones, more axons and better myelination result in the creation of an intelligent child.

PART III

<u>CHILDHOOD/PRESCHOOL</u>

By the time the child reaches the age of three, he has already learnt to walk and run fast. He already carries a large amount of information about his environment, family, and society. He has acquired sufficient language skills for his daily socio-emotional needs. He identifies his well-wishers and maintains close relations with them. He trusts people who take care of him. Naturally, he develops more intimacy with his mother.

The child who is freely allowed to explore his environment during the exploratory stage will have enough confidence to approach anything without suspicion or doubt, though he is limited with his flimsy body. By the time he passes the age of three, he has more dynamic physical and intellectual capabilities. This is the time the child is sent to preschool. At school, he gets plenty of opportunities to explore new concepts, ideas, objects, and people. The desire he had developed to fly around the world during the crawling stage is fulfilled during the preschool stage. Like a butterfly that flies from one flower to another, the child swings from one place and to another expanding his memory for deeper understanding of the world.

During this stage, children possess a lot of energy. They dig into everything and try to make meaning out of it based on the incomplete information in the brain. To an adult, a child's attitude appears naive. However, an adult can also behave like a child if he does not have enough information or his brain does not process it correctly. The key to become a successful adult depends on the quality of information one receives from family, school, and society.

When a child with ample exposure from his parents reaches school, he will be excited to see many children of his age to play with, mother-like teachers to guide him, and large open spaces to play around. His curiosity and enthusiasm skyrocket. He is thrilled to see the possibilities of playing and learning.

The child in the school seems to have so much confidence that he is ready to do anything in the world that the teachers and friends demand. The task of teachers are so simple that they just need to heed and feed to the enthusiasm, confidence, and curiosity of these children. If children at this age are not encouraged to imagine and do as they foresee, they will soon lose confidence in themselves. With each restriction, they will feel as if they have done something wrong. With repeated restrictions, they think they are not capable. When teachers and parents scold them, they repent. When scolding is repeated, it leads to guilt. Soon, they will lose interest, enthusiasm, and curiosity in everything. It may lead them to do things in secrecy and cause them to withdraw.

Appreciation is a steroid to make a child smart. Prepare to congratulate your child whenever he does something positive. What he has done might be a silly thing for an adult, but to a child, it would be a great achievement. Each appreciation from an adult doubles up the concordance of the child. Your child may be very intelligent, but that alone does not guarantee his success. First of all, he needs self-confidence to go through the paths of creativity and innovation.

Children long for appreciation from anyone they meet, especially from authority figures like parents and teachers. If they are not appreciated for a task, they get discouraged immediately and the enthusiasm and interest die out. If they are criticised, they withdraw. Criticisms give a message that the children are unworthy and incapable. Repeated criticisms reinforce and cement this negative belief about themselves. They may live with this false belief all their lives.

A child encouraged to speak and do things regularly through positive reinforcement will develop unfailing confidence to persevere any tasks assigned to him. They will use all resources and mental faculties to solve problems. Such children, when they grow, will even sacrifice their lives for the purpose of human advancement. Children raised in an atmosphere of complete acceptance will grow with unfailing courage towards challenges. On the contrary, a child raised in an atmosphere of constant criticisms will lose interest in people and the world, followed by a feeling of inferiority.

They think they are not as good as others. They feel they are a failure compared with others. Each criticism underlines this dysfunctional belief and children end up with a shy personality lacking self-confidence. This negativity permeates all his thoughts and actions leading to a pessimistic attitude towards life in general. Once such negative attitude is developed, he feels hopeless and daunting.

Many people may have thought why children who have grown in the same culture show different intellectual powers. Some children become school toppers, while others fail. The truth lies in the way children are treated at home and school. Parents and peers influence children profoundly. In addition, children can be influenced through explicit and implicit messages from mass media, internet, and publications. Unfortunately, commercialised shows are easily accessible to children at their own houses. Parents though aware of the dangers, allow children to watch these programmes just to relax themselves. They compromise the children's attitude development for their comfort. Though some programmes help children develop their language skills and acquire information about the world, we don't know what hidden messages the children have internalised, which will be working like an imperceptible virus programme influencing the child unconsciously.

Electronic media influence children more deeply because children get absorbed completely in the programme whether it is a TV show, film, or a computer game. It makes them more receptive to the messages of these programmes.

People generally are more interested in scandals and sensitive news, which is often exploited by media. They sell our fear, joy, doubts, sadness, disgust, and horror through their shows. By the time we wake up the next day, the damage to our thoughts is already done. The same is true with children too. The fact is that the children are more vulnerable because they don't have adequate information to distinguish between right and wrong. They fully believe in what they see and hear. The choice is in the hands of the parents. The parents must choose programmes that do not distort the children's cognitive skills.

Humans ability to solve different problems encountered is the sum of the information he carries in his brain about his environment, people, non-animate objects, and his own experiences and how he processes these information logically. The same information is processed differently by different people getting different results. It is because people process data differently on the basis of the capacity of their brains, biological condition, cultural beliefs, ethnicity, nationality, and religious beliefs. For example, a child raised in a culture that upholds scientific truth will approach every problem logically. The same child may behave differently in a religious society. Therefore, what is told, taught, and shown makes a man. Tell the child every day that God is omnipotent, He has created the world, we have to follow His words unquestioningly; as a result, the child will learn to passively accept everything said to him. His faculty of thinking will never develop. Anything that is forced to accept without proper analysis is an undigested piece of information that retards the natural development of humans' infinite thinking capacity, which distinguishes humans from all other animals.

Like intellectual development, personality development also

begins at school stage. Personality development is as important as intellectual growth because an intelligent child without the right attitude cannot utilise it. Personality is the way people think, feel, and behave constantly. Right thought is key to right behaviour. Children learn behaviour of parents through imitation. When you scold him with the intention of correcting him, he learns that scolding is the way to correct people. When you beat him to discipline him, he learns that beating is the way to correct others. In other words, your child will be using the same techniques against you when you grow old. I am not saying that scolding or beating is bad, but children will imbibe it. Anything that is shown to them will be absorbed like water in a sponge; it will become part of their consciousness. In the end, it will show up in their behaviour.

Being bad-tempered ourselves, we cannot expect our child to become Gauthama Buddha. He is observing how we behave with our spouse, parents, and neighbours. When we get angry, we think, "If you don't obey me, I'll get mad, I'll destroy everything, I'll frighten you to get things done my way." You don't need to say this aloud for your child to understand. Children have an internal mechanism to decipher implied meanings and read body language. After all, body language speaks volumes about a person more than words do.

Though it is possible to correct children without scolding or beating, often we have no time, patience, skill, or knowledge to execute it creatively and effectively. Negative reinforcement like scolding and beating can be effectively employed to discourage bad habits without hurting them physically and mentally. Often, mental trauma is more harmful to children in the long term due to post traumatic effects.

When we scold children, generally, we say, "What a stupid person you are? How were you born to me? You should not have been born at all, you just a burden to everyone. See how your friend Jupiter performing. He has got A+ for all subjects. I'll rip your head apart. Get lost. How can you become so foolish? I've lost all hope in you. You will never grow up etc." When you abuse your child this way, you are indirectly telling him that he is incapable and unworthy. He will be easily convinced of what you call him and live with this belief all through his remaining life and behaving accordingly. In a nutshell, you are in the process of making a real moron.

One can make a child foolish or wise. Tell an intelligent child repeatedly that he is a fool, he will become a fool. Indirect messages that you hide under words and reveal through body language are more powerful than actual words you speak because body language cannot be manipulated. Actual spoken words can be consciously chosen to give a false impression but not body language because it occurs unconsciously that you have no conscious control over.

So, what is the right way of scolding and beating? Scolding, if any, should be directed at the mistake committed by the child with patient intention of correcting and improving him, rather than the parent venting anger and satisfying his ego. Anger and rational thinking do not go together. Where there is anger, there is no logic, and vice versa. Often, when we get angry with our children, we deliberately ignore many facts pertaining to them: they are so young, they cannot be as responsible as elders, they cannot be naturally motivated to do school works or other household work, they naturally love to eat, play, and grow up, their attention span is very short compared with adults', and they are not mature enough to understand the seriousness of the task at hand (everything is child's play to him).

You say, "see how careless and irresponsible he is. Don't think I have no other works to do." And then you take a stick and beat him till you feel sorry for him. Understand the child. Scolding and beating will only help develop negative emotions, like fear, sadness, disgust, and anger, in him. Replace it with positive emotions, like confidence, joy, admiration, pleasure, and kindness. Find ways to get things done in a positive way. Offer him something as a reward that he likes most. It will often be something inexpensive, like watering plants, watching cartoons, going to a park, a toy, or a chocolate. Tell him if he finishes the assigned task in time he will get a pink ice cream with chocolate flavours. Coax him. Use all your resources and creativity to lure him. Once he yields to your enchantments, one by one, he will complete his task as you wished. Once the character is formed, he will do everything on his own without any compulsion as the external reward is replaced by self-motivation. Till then, it is parents' duty to row the boat slowly and steadily to the intended destination.

Criticism is an inevitable part of a child's progress. When a child does something wrong, somebody must correct him. However, just saying "You are wrong. Don't repeat it." won't work. The child should be logically convinced why he is wrong. Only then the idea will register in his long-term memory. We do things after processing information and the experiences are stored in our brains. When a child is restricted with a big "NO", no new information is copied to his brain. As a result, most probably, he will repeat the same mistake in the same way. Patiently, if you can call the child, seat him in your lap, and tell him why he is wrong and the advantages of not doing unsocial acts, there is a higher chance that the child remembers his mistake and does not repeat it. In addition, through this method, you are building skills of logical thinking, imagination, memory, and language, and more importantly, the right attitude. Constructive criticism should always be directed at the child's mistake rather than at the child himself. Adorn your criticism with sweet words and soothing sounds so the child does not feel upset by your remarks. In other words, when you criticise the child's mistake, you must praise him also like "Dear child, I'm very sorry to say this. I know you are a good child, but you are you tearing books and strewing it here and there. Aren't you wasting paper and making your room messy?" Follow this way to correct the child without hurting him. You are implying that the child is good and only what he has done is wrong. Such criticisms will reiterate his belief about him as a worthy, intelligent, and smart child.

Sometimes, corporal punishments like beating with a cane is also inevitable. Before discussing the right way of punishments, let us investigate the way we generally beat children. When we find something irritating from the child, a hormone called adrenaline is released in our body, our face reddens, our heart pumps blood into veins, each cell in our body is filled with extra energy, we shiver with anger, and we feel like tearing the child apart and pasting him on the wall. We shout, look around, take something solid, catch the child, and beat him till our energy is fully spent. The poor child. The same body mechanism happens in him also. He shivers with fear. When the child is frightened, he learns to be fearful. Repeated terror will gradually steal his spontaneity, cheerfulness, happiness, enthusiasm, confidence, curiosity, and courage. Parents have rightful intention to improve the child. However, once they are under the control of adrenaline, they lose their capacity to think rationally. That is why, often after beating the child, the parents feel remorse. The fact is that the imperceptible shock to the child's unconscious mind can dilute the spontaneous growth of his personality. When we beat children or get angry with them, the emotion we have raised in them is fear. This will become a habit. These children live in constant fear and begin to fear everything in the world. They live only as a shadow of their real selves, never realising their true self and inborn abilities. It is like hammering a nail into the wall and think that all the injuries caused by the nail can be solved just by removing it. However, the truth is that damage done cannot be undone. Even the best mason cannot repair it as it was before the damage. Moreover, when you are beating the child, you are teaching him that beating is okay and being beaten up is also okay. He will give you back what you have given to him when you become old. When your child is weak, you beat him. You have no patience to understand him. It is not your fault; you learnt it from your parents. These ideas are passed from generation to generation. We never dare to think on our own about the authenticity of cultural beliefs. We say, "My parents did it to me. They couldn't be wrong."

The difference between a child and an adult is in the quantity and quality of information stored in one's brain. In that sense, a 50-year-old can be called a child and a 5-year-old can be mature.

So, what is the right way of punishing a child if it is inevitable? Children are generally afraid of canes. So beating with a stick can be an easy solution to many parents and teachers to discipline a child. However, among all sections of people, disciplining means harassment: parents leap on kids, catch them tightly by hands, shaking violently, and brutally beat them. If parents want to use corporal punishments as a means of reinforcement, make sure that parents are not angry and that the children are not frightened. Make an agreement with him that if you find him tearing paper again, he will receive a beat on his palm. Corporal punishments like beating should be the last option. Instead, things that children hate to do can be used as negative reinforcement. Suppose your child, like children generally, doesn't like to write; ask him to write a few sentences (alphabets or words with young children) as negative reinforcement; let him choose writing or beating. If he chooses beating, you are beating him with his permission; he is experiencing the pain willingly, which would not hurt his consciousness. It will only develop his determination to improve himself. Moreover, he will try to overcome the fear of beating. It will develop his courage and skill to manage such unpleasant situations in future. If he prefers writing, he is stimulating his brain. Soon, writing will become his favourite activity. In both ways, the child gets benefited. Understanding of the mistakes and accepting of punishments will gradually make a child self-disciplined.

Parental behaviour towards their children, including body language, choice of words, and tone, can largely influence the personality of children. If parents want their child to trust others, the parents must first be truthful to them. Parents employ many shortcuts to get tasks done quickly by the child. You want your child to eat food by himself. Suppose, he is not listening to you.

You say, "Dear son, if you take milk quickly, I will take you to the park." The child is excited by the promise and finishes it quickly. Later, the parent gets busy in completing his professional work and is unable to take the child to the park. The child gets disappointed. Next time when you give a promise, the child will suspect your sincerity and he may not do the task with the same enthusiasm as he did before. If this manipulation is continued in different situations by the other members of the family, friends, and teachers, he grows up suspicious of people and their motives. It can affect the growth of his personality. He may not be able to establish and maintain relationships.

Whenever somebody approaches him with good intentions, he will doubt them; he will think they are trying to manipulate, cheat, trick, or loot him. People keep away from such people who distrust them for anything and everything. This results in isolation. Isolation can trigger mental tensions like nervousness, fear, anger, irrational and illogical beliefs, uncontrolled emotions, depression, and psychosomatic illnesses.

Some parents have full trust in their children that their kids will surely mature, become responsible, learn good behaviour, become generous, become selfless, become knowledgeable, and learn to manage their emotions. The most important idea is our expectation that our child will ultimately improve. It is a fact that all children will one day become an adult only if elders allow them to become one. We cannot expect a child to behave like an adult does. To become an adult, he must first pass the childhood stage. Nobody can skip any stage. Children crawl before they walk; they walk before they run. We were all children once. What we are today is what our parents thought of us as kids. What your child will be is what you think of your child today. If you have full trust in your child that they will become responsible one day, the child will grow to be responsible. If you think your child will never mature, you are right. Your belief will become a self-fulfilling prophecy.

One of the unscientific technique adults use to correct the young ones is ridicule and sarcasm. We address children, "Is this the way to do it you fool?" Elders speak so to ventilate their sprouting anger than to correct the youngster's mistake. It does more harm than it does good. Children lose their positive belief about themselves. (Often, success in the new world is based on our belief about capabilities rather than actual capabilities. Interestingly, this little capability is enough to be called as above average in this century. A little of human brain is capable of extraordinary achievements.) Our self-concept is formed of others' reactions towards us in different situations. If everyone praises us all the time, we become proud of ourselves and our self-esteem increases. If we are criticised for whatever we do, we think negatively of ourselves, which results in an inferiority complex, which depletes our self-esteem. The development of self-esteem is key to personality growth. Children growing in an environment of praise, appreciation, affection, recognition, tolerance, and trust will grow with self-esteem, and consequently, a positive attitude towards everything. Each successful attempt increases the self-esteem of the child and gives him enough confidence to embrace the next task. It goes on and on reciprocally complementing each other. In the same way, a child who loses all the time loses his confidence and develops an inferiority complex.

Parents should appreciate initiatives by the children despite the results. Complete acceptance by the parent will boost the confidence of the child. Praise their efforts not the results. It will motivate them to attempt repeatedly despite the constant failures, which are normal in the learning process. Tell them, "You have done your best, that's great. Keep on doing it. You will succeed." Never say, "You have wasted my time and energy, muddle head, how many times I have told you? You careless, see how your friends have done it, look here you bum." Though the intention is good, negative criticisms will make the child doubtful of his own abilities overtime. Later, they will try to avoid situations that they think will invite criticism and ridicule. Finally, they will lose enthusiasm and interest in doing any work. They shy away from people and end up isolated. Repeated failures followed by negative criticisms will eventually stagnate their natural growth and development.

Children raised in an atmosphere of shame and fear will try to avoid them through lies and deceit. At any cost, they try to get away from elders' unpleasant comments. Parents who appreciate and reward children only when they behave as per their expectations tend to be manipulative as they will try to win games through any means. Parents who appreciate children for their best efforts despite the results tend to have a positive attitude towards all tasks. They will internalise in the children that efforts are more important than the results. They are not bothered about the consequences of the efforts. They think whether they fail or not they are going to get appreciated. Such children are found to be successful in later life.

Children without confidence will depend on others for doing anything and everything. They will be afraid of taking a decision by themselves. They believe that they are not intelligent or mature enough to make their own choices. Even when they grow up, they will be habituated to hide behind somebody and speak only over others' shoulders. Such children seem to be anxious when they are alone. They want to cling to someone they trust. As dependency is a temporary option, it will lead to tension over time. Dependent children will be poor in academic performance because of their inability to concentrate on the task at hand. This anxiety will become a habit and follows them in their adulthood causing all types of personality disorders. These unfortunate children may be written off as failures or unnecessary burden by society and family. Finally, people will say, "See, he has had everything but he hasn't utilised it properly." In the end, nobody bothers about the improper parenting that actually caused the child to become a dependant person.

Some parents are too strict with their children, and they expect them to be obedient all the time. They simply ask children to do this and that. They want them not to speak this and that. They behave like maharajas whose orders cannot be violated. Parents think their young ones are incapable of thinking of their own. The parents firmly believe that obedience without questioning is the way to teach discipline. However, by the time children reach the age of five, they begin to question, at least in their mind, the demands of the parents. This is the time children's logical skills develop. They understand that their parents' demands are not justified. It causes confusion and frustration in them. They bury their fury deep in their mind. Some children behave defensively, but become submissive owing to their physical limitations. Forced obedience may explode in the form of violence or unsocial behaviour later during adolescent stage.

Children raised in an atmosphere of unjustified demands may bring out all the regressed anger in the form of self-mutilation, violence, and anti-social behaviour. They may hit their head and knees on the wall or shatter household items in temper. They lose faith in social rules, cultural principles, and constitutional laws. They have an urge to violate rules as a protest against the unfair treatment they were subjected to as children at the hands of their parents. If proper guidance is not given later in school and colleges, there is every chance that the children turn to become anti-social personalities.

It is very important to treat children as if they were grownups. Don't try to exploit their physical weakness. Whenever you make a demand to children, make sure it is justified. The best way to make your child do your demand is to show it yourself first. Children learn many things by imitating influential people. Parents, teachers, and friends influence them a lot. Some parents have little respect for their children though they sincerely long for them becoming great and successful. They believe that children should be submissive and never dare to question the authority of parents as they did with their parents. (They claim they are successful. They ask others to look up to them. They firmly believe that their success is because of their parents. However, they don't know they would have been a different personality if they had been looked after by parents differently.) The truth is   , only an intelligent child can question. If there is any merit in his questioning, instead of feeling insulted, take it as an opportunity to engage in a meaningful conversation with him. If the child is wrong, convince him why he is wrong. You may fail in your attempt to convince him. Nevertheless, do it. You may fail hundreds of times. Still, keep doing it. Have faith in your child that one day, he will understand. This firm belief is what makes a child mature and smart. This way, the child trusts his parents, other members of family, and society. Such children, when they grow up, respect and follow social laws, customs, and culture. He knows the necessity of such rules even though they seem absurd. Such children will democratically try to modify laws if they are against equity and justice.

Parents who are overprotective physically and emotionally will have children who cannot manage stress from external sources, like schools, colleges, courts, and other social institutions. These parents too yield to the demand of the children. They fulfil all the desires of the children without thinking about the consequences. The children's sensual satisfaction is important to them over intellectual development. Such children, when they grow up, expect everyone to behave like their parents did. Once they enter social life outside their house, they cannot adjust to the role they have to play. Maintaining interpersonal relationships will become a difficult task for them. They may manipulate others emotionally to yield them to their demands. They cannot sustain a relationship because they easily get upset even by the slightest behavioural changes in others. As they have not been trained in managing emotions, they either become extremely exuberant or depressed, fluctuating from one emotion to another. They will be labelled as too childish. They may abruptly argue with others and snap the relationship. They may show contempt when they see you next time. They do all these with their friends, colleagues, spouse, and everyone they meet as they did successfully with their parents. For example, if your spouse closes the door noisily, locks it and remains inside moaning for hours; it is a part of their manipulative techniques they employed in their childhood. Don't blame or get angry with them; they are showing only the behaviour developed by their parents, who were over-protective, emotional, and yielding themselves.

 Parents should yield to demands only if children are right and positive. If they are wrong, explain to them why. Personality is developed through the messages they come across daily. The messages children receive may not have an immediate effect as parents expect, but it will not be lost completely. Anything that goes into the brain is never completely lost. The synthesis of all information they have received over time will form part of one's personality one day. Every parent must have this expectation from their children. Otherwise, they will make immediate negative conclusions about themselves about who they are. Children should internalise the fact that their every demand is not worthy and that they need to adapt to the expectations of the society by controlling their emotions. Children must experience the value of both negative and positive emotions. They must learn to manage their emotions positively but not manipulate them negatively. Children's logical and rational thinking skills should be developed through meaningful discussions. Children whose logical and rational thinking skills are developed early are found to be emotionally mature and able to comfortably deal with stress provoking situations.

We often ignore children's need of recognition and respect, which play an important role in the formation of self-image, self-concept, and self-esteem in children. If a child has a positive concept of self, self-esteem develops in him. Self-esteem is the base for growing up towards a socially acceptable personality. Self-concept develops through the responses of others towards us. When we receive positive responses, and we form a positive concept of ourselves. When others respect you, you feel you are respectable. When others show their love and affection towards you, you feel you are worthy as a person. On the contrary, when your opinions are ignored, you feel you are not important and capable. Such recurrent negative comments from others form inferiority complexes in us, which increases the chance of disillusionment and mental illnesses later.

How do you respond when your child asks you something? Do you feel like they are disturbing you? Do you feel disturbed by his constant nagging? Do you say that you are busy and keep away? Do you ask him to ask somebody else? If answers to all these questions are "yes", you are delaying his growth or putting off his curiosity or injecting inferiority complex.

If you sincerely long to grow your child into a capable person, first you must change your attitude towards him. Attitude is the value you assign to people and things you meet. Trust your child like a prince, speak to him like he is a wise old owl, respond to him as if the world cannot sustain without him. At the same time, criticise his mistakes, not the child personally, with the intention of improving him. This way the child will grow into a wise prince.

Every child in their formative years tests his position in the family by participating in various activities around the house. This is part of growing up. Recognition of their attitude will accelerate their overall development. Negligence will stagnate their progress. Moreover, their desire to get recognition may get fixated, and when they grow up, their unfulfilled desire for recognition takes an ugly turn, and they become a nuisance in public. Attention seeking disorder is the result of negligence during childhood. Others immediately realise the empty responses of such people and further ignore them, which further deteriorates their already dilapidated self-concept. It will move in an unstoppable vicious circle of negative feelings and end up in maladaptive personality disorders.

Children regress all the frustrations they experience during childhood. Some parents are very strict with their children and treat them like mechanical devices. Then never compromise on anything and ignore the emotional needs of children. These parents are determined to make them something that they could not become themselves. They are not satisfied with what they do. Often, they focus their whole attention on a small error in the work. They don't care about appreciating the child's effort in the work. Each time he proudly shows his work to the parent, the child gets disappointed with the response. Finally, the child also begins to doubt his abilities and is never satisfied with himself. Whenever he does something, he thinks negatively. When he somehow gets over this, there comes another and another. It goes on. In the end, he is totally confused and unable to reach a consensus to finish the work and ends up worse than he was. Such children are never satisfied with anything in their life. They constantly criticise others and never complete a work. They live a life of continuous frustration and unhappiness.

Parents should focus more on children's abilities, not much on their weaknesses. Each time, notwithstanding the result, if a child is appreciated, he will grow with a positive attitude towards everything. He will understand that life's successes and joys are the result of improving one's strengths rather than focusing on weaknesses. They learn that "to human is err but to forgive is divine." They help others identify their strong areas and motivate them to work on these. They learn that humans are different from other animals because they can change their behaviour, attitude, and beliefs with effort. They learn that there are many ways of doing a single thing. They know that people differ from one another on the basis of their ethnicity, education, nationality, and culture. They also know that everybody is similar in the sense that humans are capable of thinking positively, helping others, and growing stronger, in addition to overthinking negatively, being selfish, and being weak.

Perfectionism is an illusion because nothing in the world is perfect and nothing in the world can become so. However, striving for perfection is logical because through this, we improve our knowledge, skills, and behaviour. Children should be encouraged to work hard and persevere. Their success is in their efforts, not in the results. If they are able to enjoy the work they do, they are successful. Any bitter task can be converted into an enjoyable fest through complete acceptance and continuous appreciation. Some parents are like ice: they melt before their children's demands. It is only a matter of an innocent looking request from them, and the parents lay down themselves. Such children grow with the belief that people can be easily made to yield to their plans. They develop superiority complex like a narcissist. They think they are superior to others in all respects and so should be obeyed and respected. They exploit people who are lenient, yielding, and naive. They find ways to force others to their purpose. If they don't obey, a narcissist will threaten and seek revenge. They cannot accept any kind of disapproval. Disapprovals, disrespect, unrecognition, disobedience, and authority put them down as they are not used to it. Their parents never gave them chances to experience emotions of loss or their own limitations. They believe that they have God-like powers, and others are their devotees. They think their ideas are the best and final and so cannot be questioned. If somebody questions, they cannot adjust to the setback; they will have an emotional outburst. Often, they find it difficult to maintain a sincere and social relationships with others. They turn a deaf ear towards the emotions of others. To them, the result is more important than the means to reach there. Their obsessive compulsive "do or die" attitude heeds no attention to the emotions of individuals, and they end up mobilising people against them.

Everybody loves their children very much. If they don't, they must. However, parents' responsibility is not just to satisfy the children's sensibility, but their cognition too. Some essential skills, like social interaction, interpersonal relations, knowing one's strengths and weaknesses, cultural code of conduct, national expectations, desired behaviours, various emotions, and their management should be taught. Wherever children are found wrong and their demands naive, parents should have the heart to say NO firmly followed by explanations why they are wrong. As a psychologist rightly said, children should be given the vitamin 'N' tablet sometimes.

Every parent sincerely wishes his child to grow into a great personality with optimum development. To get there, parents should ensure that their home environment is free of stress and fear. Some parents frighten their children in the name of discipline. However, repeated exposure to a fearful environment causes the child to fear similar situations. Children who are stressed and frightened a lot in childhood develop fear for social situations. They try to escape from presentations and group discussions and avoid assertive communication. They appear timid and diffident growing backward and inward.

 An example to understand the peculiar way our mind works is ghost stories, religious beliefs, and all other unscientific ideas children learn during early years. These stories scared and excited them. These feelings of fear, excitement, and beliefs remain intact even in their old age despite the scientific education they receive. All the scientific information received later in their lives is not enough to erase the superstitious beliefs they learnt during childhood. That is why, early years are a crucial period as far as children's intellectual and emotional development is concerned. Tell children the truth, they will become truthful, they will rewrite the entire history of lies, they will convince others why their beliefs are unscientific, they will not be enticed by the illusion of realities and fantasies. They will also conduct research before believing in anything. They grow upward and lead the world forward.

Every time parents show their anger, they scare the children. From an evolutionary point of view, fear evolved to protect us from potentially dangerous situations. When our ancestors lived in the forest, this emotion helped them stay away from wild animals or wild fires. When fear is aroused, our brain assumes that something is wrong and prepares our body and mind to defend against it at any cost. If the general atmosphere at home is fearful, children will be habituated to be in a fearful mood even if there is nothing to be afraid of. Later in life, it will be reproduced in all situations, even in non-threatening ones. They will appear to be timid, tense, and shy. Instead of employing fear as a basic technique to manage children, parents can offer rewards, internal and external, to develop them.

We can assume the mental state of a child who has been brought up through manipulation by his parents with the intention of correcting or escaping from his naughtiness. Parents tell him lies, make him believe the existence of fictional characters, and force him to obey irrational orders. This child grows with seeds of hallucinations and delusions that flower later in adulthood.

Parents may have noticed that, in many occasions, their children, when they are given a task or not completed one, they defend themselves with several excuses, lies, and cooked-up stories. Children lie not because they are born liars but because they are afraid of punishment and humiliation at your hands. To save themselves from injuries, physical and mental, they resort to many defensive mechanisms, which gradually incapacitate them. Later in their adulthood, they withdraw to fantasies, daydreams, drugs, and other substances. They were not used to success in any field, so they are afraid to take up any challenge. They learnt that avoidance is the easy way of adjustment. These children have never been taught to adjust, and thus, cannot adapt. Thus, maladjustment develops in them.

All human success is because of their ability to adapt to their environment and their intelligence to create their own environment as per their needs. Anybody who cannot adjust to their environment is destined to fail. They instead substitute unreality with reality through fantasising. That is why, despite the education of parents, culture, ethnicity, time, and place, some children deviate from usual courses of life and become maladaptive. If we are living happily now, it is because we have hope in the next day. However, if we are doubtful of our abilities, we lose confidence in everything. All the positive qualities, especially confidence, are developed during childhood. If parents can build confidence in children before they are six, they have won.

If children are ignored in childhood, they will assume that they are inferior and unworthy to be considered for anything. Their desire to get love, respect, and recognition will be fixed at this stage. When they become adults, they will become a public nuisance by behaving inappropriately trying to get attention every now and then. They poke their head in every pot not meant for them. When they are ignored, they will be shocked with inordinate temper tantrums. This temper makes them lose their emotional control, causing an anxious and unsatisfied life. This in turn makes them introverts and recluses escaping from social challenges causing various phobias. As all these happen in a vicious circle, the person falls into depression with other associated problems like suicidal tendencies and drug addiction.

With lenient parents, children grow with the belief that everyone and everything can be manipulated and made to obey them without questioning as their parents would. Lenient parents behave like the *djinn* in Arabian stories, ever ready to serve the young ones. Such children learn that everyone is like the djinn to serve and please them always. Such children face adjustment problems in adulthood with authority figures, like parents, teachers, bosses, and senior colleagues. They don't like anybody making them angry or dissatisfied because they have never experienced refusal and negative criticism. To them, anything that satisfies their instinct is good and acceptable; anything that restricts their desires is unacceptable. They were not exposed to various social situations to internalise the unwritten cultural norms or various roles and powers enjoyed by people in various positions.

Children of authoritarian parents, as they are constrained time and again unreasonably, exhibit authoritarian behaviour towards their subordinates once they are in a higher position. Such children were tarnished, harassed, humiliated, and criticised a lot to the point of losing their self-esteem. (All people prefer death to losing their self-esteem. They may go to any extent to keep their self-esteem.) When they are in a high position, they cannot tolerate a word intended to question their authority.

They often threaten their subordinates for simple mistakes. Such anti-social behaviour is caused by their superiority complex. They think, "I have suffered a lot when I was nobody. I cannot tolerate it anymore, especially at the hands of my subordinates. I will teach everybody a lesson." They belittle others to elevate themselves psychologically instead of advancing themselves.

Children should be dealt with carefully. Your body language, choice of words, tone of voice, and implied meanings all influence the character of your child. Most importantly, parents must ensure that they always speak and act logically. Any illogical ideas and actions by the parents are accepted by children as logical and rational, and the children will employ the same logic everywhere all through their lives. Belief systems are very difficult to change at later stages in life. In childhood, children can be easily fooled by your ideas; they always accept them as facts without proper thinking.

Children raised in an atmosphere of deception, cunningness, lies, illogicality, irrationality, and authoritarianism are found to have some kind of bizarreness later in life. They will be despised and avoided by others for being unsocial. These repeated rejections will further make them stick to the old ways of dealing with problems and further go away from the right path. Ultimately, they will begin to doubt their capabilities and fall into depression. Consequently, they resort to shortcuts, like alcohol, drugs, and tobacco, to create an illusion of reality and to find happiness. As these substances cannot give long-term satisfaction, they become dependant on them and become addicted. All credit goes to the parents for their parenting skills!

Children always imitate their parents. They observe and learn how parents cope with different situations in life. If parents appear to be angry, anxious, and depressed, children also become so. If parents turn to alcohol to manage their problems, children presumably follow suit. Once shortcuts like drinking are adopted as a method of coping with problems, people cannot come out of it. They gradually loose friends, family, and jobs. It further forces them to embrace more drugs. The initiation of all problems can be traced back to bad parenting that promotes doubt, fear, inferiority, manipulation, illogicality, and violence.

Many phobias develop during childhood. Parents with uncontrollable emotions, doubts, and superstitions cause an environment that causes children to develop different irrational fears of open spaces, closed spaces, authority, people, and public speaking. Fear for parents can be converted into different forms, like fear of spiders, cockroaches, and dogs. Phobias can be triggered by real incidents or imaginary ones as in a dream. For instance, you have scolded and beaten your child for his naughtiness; in sleep, this frightening experience may transformed into different experiences like the child being chased by a dog or falling into a pit or drowning in an ocean. After this dream, he may develop a fear for buffaloes, dogs, heights, or water. Therefore, creating a positive atmosphere that instils trust, courage, and empathy through acceptance, guidance, motivation, appreciation, and love can prevent personality disorders and phobias.

A child can be said to be growing well only when his physical, emotional, cognitive, and social needs are taken care of. Balanced food builds body and brain properly. Brian development influences our logic, reason, and thoughts. Our logic and thoughts influence our emotions, and vice versa.

Similar situations can be interpreted differently by different people based on the way they think. When a teacher scolds his students for something, some children take it positively and get motivated to work hard. At the same time, some take it negatively, become tense, and get demotivated. All because of the way they think. In the same way, emotions, social development, and cognition are interconnected and influence each other on the go. A child with the knowledge of various emotions, their functions, and experience to manage them is found to be more logical, rational, confidant, intelligent, and healthy. Such children develop self-esteem, and they don't shy away from social settings. They freely interact with others and learn more about behaviour, culture, and social norms, which further enhances their personality. Thus, children will move in the right direction regarding their physical, emotional, social, and cognitive development: the direction of the momentum is often decided by the directions given by the parents.

So, the first six years of a child is a crucial period of his mental development. It does not happen naturally. It is created by elders, mainly parents. That is why parenting is the most difficult job in the world. It is easy to ignore. It is difficult to show patience and perseverance for a long period of six years. Nothing in the world is done without constant efforts. You may be busy in building your business. But, if you are serious as a parent regarding the future of your child, find time to nurture your child through affection and guidance.

Development of values is also interconnected with cognitive and socio-emotional development. At early stages, children do not have enough information in their brain to assess the value of moral principles prevalent in society. So, children comply blindly. Their compliance is out of fear of punishment. They know that if they break the norms, they will be punished. They don't know why they should obey them. Knowledgeable parents know this fact and so explain the logic behind each rule from very early stage itself. The parents' interaction may not bring any immediate change in the children's behaviour, but in the long run, they will make sense to them. Such children, who are told the underlying facts and beliefs behind norms and code of conduct, develop their cognitive abilities fast owing to the quantity and quality of information in their brain followed by moral thinking and compliance. Such children are found to be humble and obedient to their parents, teachers, and others.

Initially, children obey rules without questioning for fear of punishments and criticisms; in later stages, they follow rules because they know why rules are necessary. They may question the validity of some rules that seem against the fundamental nature of life. They reach this stage by comparing their past experiences with existing information. In this process, if they find any dissonance, they may resist to obey the rule. They may go to such an extent as to correct and improve the rule democratically. Children who grow in an atmosphere of free speech and acceptance achieve moral maturity much faster than those living in an atmosphere of compulsion and nagging criticisms.

<u>COGNITIVE DEVELOPMENT</u>

Socratic question is one of the techniques that can be used to build cognitive abilities of children. In this technique, children are asked general questions to contradict their thinking pattern. They reflect on their own thoughts and come up with more logical thoughts. This way, children will develop higher order thinking skills. In addition, it will improve children's analytical and logical thinking skills, which are the basis for self-actualisation. This technique can be used when the child begins to understand languages. In the beginning, elders may lose interest in these types of brain teasers as they are not getting a quick response they expected from kids. However, parents with ample patience, perseverance, and trust will certainly succeed.

Learning happens through reflection when children get new information about a thing through self-observation, experience, or interaction with others. When a parent deliberately asks a question to the child with the intention of adding a list of new information to the mind of the child, the child adds this new information to the old one and forms a new thought. This way, parents indirectly transfer new information into the child letting him think logically by himself. This method creates curiosity, interest, and a liking for learning in children and strengthens their biological as well as psychological capabilities. Nowadays, many parents, instead of making efforts to help children reflect, which seems a time consuming and frustrating task to them, let children obey them without explaining the underlying reason and logic of the order. This cramming is in no way going to help children's cognitive development.

Games for Cognitive Development

Games that stimulate children's brain are useful in developing their cognitive capacities. A few popular games for brain development are explained below:

1. Leaves and Shape: Collect leaves from different trees or plants and ask the child to arrange according to their shape or size. Offer rewards for successful completion of the task. The same game may be played with any other available articles, like pebbles, stones, clothes, pens, blocks, and pictures.

2. Colour: Gather some objects of different colours and ask the child to group them by colour. For example, objects of white colour should be grouped together, and so on.

3. Hide and Seek: Hide objects in different areas of the house and ask children to find them. Give some clues. Let the child interpret the clues.

4. Chess: Board games like chess can boost logical, decision-making, problem–solving, and analytical skills.

5. Video Games: Many educational games available on play stores can stimulate children's brain. The games that are only for entertainment are not recommended as they may have a reverse effect. The games that induce children's problem-solving skills, imagination, and psychomotor skills can help.

6. Carom Board and other Indoor Games: These games not only develop psychomotor movements but also spatial intelligence.

7. Drawings: Most children like to draw and sketch. Encourage them to scribble their imagination. Later, it will turn into creativity.

8. Paper Craft and Clay Modelling: Teach children the possibilities of making models of different objects using paper and clay, which are easily available and inexpensive. Give them the freedom to manipulate them and satisfy their curious and naughty minds.

9. Rubik's Cube: It is an excellent game for children to stimulate their brains. Hand–brain coordination, dexterity, speed, analytical skill, logical skill, colour identification, and concentration can be developed through this game. Let them solve it without the aid of some readymade formulae.

10. Building Blocks: Safe sets of blocks are available in the market, or wooden blocks of different shapes can be made at home. It can develop children's imagination, creativity, and recognition of shape and colour.

11. Puzzles: It can boost children's logical, analytical, problem–solving, and decision-making skills. In puzzles, children initially use trial and error method to solve them. Later, they do it through thinking and insight formation.

12. Role Play: Children have a natural tendency to imitate elders. Let children enact the roles of their mother, father, teachers, and friends. Let them make use of available household items in the

game. This game can develop their social skills, imagination, and creativity.

13. Musical Instruments: Any new activity can stimulate different areas of the brain. Learning to play a musical instrument develops untapped areas of the brain, hand–brain coordination, and musical skills. Einstein loved to play the violin.

14. Languages: Teach children as many languages as possible. Children who grow in a multilingual family/society are found to be smarter than kids who learn only a single language.

14. Dancing: Dancing can develop one's bodily intelligence. It strengthens the connection between different muscle groups of the body and brain. More control children have over their muscles, better and easier employment of them is ensured in other activities.

15. Work with both Hands: Encourage children to use both hands to do the same task. Right-handed can be asked to write with the left hand, and vice versa.

16. Cooking: In addition to learning a useful skill, cooking can develop children's logical, psychomotor, and analytical skills. It will also improve their creativity and imagination. Let them be little chemists. Let them mix different vegetables and create their own experimental food. Let them taste it and change the ingredients when they make it next time.

Activities given in the book are only to give a basic idea to develop your own innovative ones. Simple tasks like these can make a sea change to the skill and IQ level of your child. Any simple activities that provide new experience can be utilised. Any material at home can be presented to children in different combinations.

AFTERWARD

In spite of what we have discussed so far about the mental and physical health of the child is equally to be taken care of as it is the base in which the mind grows. If the base is not fertile, then the mind won't grow healthy.

The best food for humans generally is pure vegetarian. Our body is more comfortable in digesting vegetables and fruits than it is with meat and eggs. Vegetarian food contains all nutrition necessary for our body in required amounts. The body can't absorb more or less from veggies than is required. This keeps the balance of our bodies and we remain healthy for a long time.

Non-vegetarian food though seems more delicious and equally nutritious can damage our internal organs quickly and inflict diseases easily. Include different types of fruits, leafy vegetables, nuts, and flowery vegetables in your child's daily menu to build a strong base for his mental and physical growth.

It is a known fact that packaged food contains poisonous metals, plastics, and chemicals, which in the long run will damage all internal organs of our body and cause cancer. An example is preparing food in aluminium plates and causing Alzheimer's disease due to aluminium deposit in the brain. In the same way, the chemicals and metals, though in small quantities, found in packaged foods will deposit in our internal organs and cause them to fail permanently.

Home food using vegetables grown at home is the best food for your body and mind. This factor will also determine the mental state and ensure its optimum development. Parents seriously need to take care of this factor also and create a habit of eating at home than from restaurants.

[1]